Microsoft®

Outlook 2000

Illustrated Essentials Edition

Marie L. Swanson
Jeff Goding

ONE MAIN STREET, CAMBRIDGE, MA 02142

Australia • Canada • Denmark • Japan • Mexico • New Zealand • Philippines
Puerto Rico • Singapore • South Africa • Spain • United Kingdom • United States

Microsoft Outlook 2000—Illustrated Essentials Edition is published by Course Technology

Senior Product Manager:	Kathryn Schooling
Product Manager:	Jennifer A. Duffy
Associate Product Manager:	Emily Heberlein
Contributing Author:	Nicole J. Pinard
Production Editor:	Elena Montillo
Developmental Editor:	Katherine T. Pinard
Composition House:	GEX, Inc.
QA Manuscript Reviewer:	John Freitas
Text Designer:	Joseph Lee, Joseph Lee Designs
Cover Designer:	Doug Goodman, Doug Goodman Designs

Trademarks

Course Technology and the Open Book logo are registered trademarks of Course Technology.

Illustrated Projects and the Illustrated Series are trademarks of Course Technology.

Some of the product names and company names used in this book have been used for identification purposes only and may be trademarks or registered trademarks of their respective manufacturers . and sellers.

Disclaimer

Course Technology reserves the right to revise this publication and make changes from time to time in its content without notice.

For more information contact:

Course Technology
One Main Street
Cambridge, MA 02142

Or find us on the Word Wide Web at: www.course.com

ISBN 0-7600-6075-4

Printed in the United States of America

1 2 3 4 5 6 7 8 9 BM 04 03 02 01 00

The Illustrated Series Offers the Entire Package for your Microsoft Office 2000 Needs

Office 2000 MOUS Certification Coverage

The Illustrated Series offers a growing number of Microsoft-approved titles that cover the objectives required to pass the Office 2000 MOUS exams. After studying with any of the approved Illustrated titles (see list on inside cover), you will have mastered the Core and Expert skills necessary to pass any Office 2000 MOUS exam with flying colors. In addition, **MOUS Certification Objectives** at the end of the book map to where specific MOUS skills can be found in each lesson and where students can find additional practice.

Helpful New Features

The Illustrated Series responded to Customer Feedback by adding a **Project Files list** at the back of the book for easy reference, Changing the red font in the Steps to green for easier reading, and Adding New Conceptual lessons to units to give students the extra information they need when learning Office 2000.

New Exciting Case and Innovative On-Line Companion

There is an exciting new case study used throughout our textbooks, a fictitious company called MediaLoft, designed to be "real-world" in nature by introducing the kinds of activities that students will encounter when working with Microsoft Office 2000. The **MediaLoft Web site**, available at www.course.com/illustrated/medialoft, is an innovative Student Online Companion which enhances and augments the printed page by bringing students onto the Web for a dynamic and continually updated learning experience. The MediaLoft site mirrors the case study used throughout the book, creating a real-world intranet site for this chain of bookstore cafés. This Companion is used to complete the WebWorks exercise in each unit of this book, and to allow students to become familiar with the business application of an intranet site.

Enhance Any Illustrated Text with these Exciting Products!

Course CBT

Enhance your students' Office 2000 classroom learning experience with self-paced computer-based training on CD-ROM. Course CBT engages students with interactive multimedia and hands-on simulations that reinforce and complement the concepts and skills covered in the textbook. All the content is aligned with the MOUS (Microsoft Office User Specialist) program, making it a great preparation tool for the certification exams. Course CBT also includes extensive pre- and post-assessments that test students' mastery of skills.

Course Assessment

How well do your students *really* know Microsoft Office? Course Assessment is a performance-based testing program that measures students' proficiency in Microsoft Office 2000. Previously known as SAM, Course Assessment is available for Office 2000 in either a live or simulated environment. You can use Course Assessment to place students into or out of courses, monitor their performance throughout a course, and help prepare them for the MOUS certification exams.

Create Your Ideal Course Package with CourseKits™

If one book doesn't offer all the coverage you need, create a course package that does. With Course Technology's CourseKits—our mix-and-match approach to selecting texts—you have the freedom to combine products from more than one series. When you choose any two or more Course Technology products for one course, we'll discount the price and package them together so your students can pick up one convenient bundle at the bookstore.

For more information about any of these offerings or other Course Technology products, contact your sales representative or visit our web site at:

www.course.com

Preface

Welcome to *Microsoft Outlook 2000— Illustrated Essentials Edition.* This highly visual book is designed to be used with Learning Outlook 2000 E-mail, a simulation program that mimics the experiences of working with the e-mail capabilities of Microsoft Outlook 2000. Using both Learning Outlook 2000 E-mail and this book, you can learn the basics of using Microsoft Outlook 2000, which would otherwise be difficult in a classroom setting. The Appendix covers additional features of Microsoft Outlook 2000 such as managing appointments, tasks, and contacts, and previewing your day.

▶ About Learning Outlook 2000 E-mail

Learning Outlook 2000 E-mail lets you learn Microsoft Outlook 2000 in a controlled environment without having to install the actual Microsoft Outlook 2000 software. The Learning Outlook 2000 E-mail program is contained in the Instructor's Resource Kit and can be installed on stand-alone machines. See the Instructor's Resource Kit page of this preface for information.

▶ About this Approach

What makes the Illustrated approach so effective at teaching software skills? It's quite simple. Each skill is presented on two facing pages, with the step-by-step instructions on the left page, and large screen illustrations on the right. Students can focus on a single skill without having to turn the page. This unique design makes information extremely accessible and easy to absorb, and provides a great reference for after the course is over. This hands-on approach also makes it ideal for both self-paced or instructor-led classes.

Each lesson, or "information display," contains the following elements:

Each 2-page spread focuses on a single skill.

Clear step-by-step directions explain how to complete the specific task, with what students are to type in green. When students follow the numbered steps, they quickly learn how each procedure is performed and what the results will be.

Concise text that introduces the basic principles discussed in the lesson. Procedures are easier to learn when concepts fit into a framework.

Starting Learning Outlook 2000 E-mail

Before you can read or send messages, you must start Outlook and enter a secret password. In this lesson and throughout this unit, you will work with the Learning Outlook 2000 E-mail program, which is installed in the Course Programs program group on the Start menu. (If you were using Microsoft Outlook, it would be installed in a different program group.) *You need to complete this unit in one sitting; do not exit Learning Outlook 2000 E-mail until instructed.* Alice needs to start Learning Outlook 2000 E-mail and sign into her mail account using a password.

Steps

1. **Click the Start button on the taskbar, point to Programs, then point to Course Programs**
   See Figure A-2. Note that the actual Microsoft Outlook program would be stored in a different program group on your computer.

   QuickTip
   Depending on how your e-mail system is set up, you may be required to follow different steps to log into your electronic mailbox.

2. **Click Learning Outlook 2000 E-mail**
   You see a message box describing the Learning Outlook 2000 E-mail simulation program.

3. **Click Continue**
   The message box describing the Learning Outlook 2000 E-mail simulation program closes, and the Learning Outlook 2000 E-mail program starts. The Enter Password dialog box appears as shown in Figure A-3. Alice Wegman is already entered as the user name. The domain name is MEDIALOFT. A domain is a collection of computers that the network manager groups together because the computers are used for the same task. The domain name MEDIALOFT is a fictional domain name. If this were your mail account, you would enter a mailbox name and domain name provided by your system administrator. On many networks, before you can use Outlook, you must enter a secret password identifying yourself.

4. **Click in the Password text box**
   Passwords are case sensitive; that is, *PASSWORD* is different from *password.*

   QuickTip
   To keep your password secret, do not write it down in a visible place, share it with others, or use a familiar or common name. Such passwords are easy for others to guess.

5. **In the Password text box, type any password you wish, using up to 19 characters, then press [Enter]**
   Four messages show up at first. After a minute, a total of nine messages appear.

CLUES TO USE
Keeping your password secure

In Learning Outlook 2000 E-mail, you can enter any password you wish using up to 19 characters. If you are on a network using Outlook, however, your system administrator will probably provide you with your own unique and secret password. After you have been assigned a password, you can then change it to one of your own choosing. It is a good idea to change your password every two months to keep it secure. Make sure you choose a password that is easy for you to remember, but difficult for others to guess. As a security benefit, your password does not appear in the Sign In dialog box as you type it. Instead, you see "*" as you type each letter.

▶ OUTLOOK A-4 **GETTING STARTED WITH OUTLOOK 2000**

Hints as well as trouble-shooting advice, right where you need it — next to the step itself.

Clues to Use boxes provide concise information that either expands on one component of the major lesson skill or describes an independent task that is in some way related to the major lesson skill.

Every lesson features large-size, full-color representations of what the students' screen should look like after completing the numbered steps.

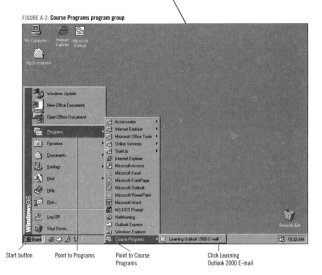

FIGURE A-2: **Course Programs program group**

Start button   Point to Programs   Point to Course Programs   Click Learning Outlook 2000 E-mail

FIGURE A-3: **Enter Password dialog box**

Enter your password here which will appear as a series of asterisks

GETTING STARTED WITH OUTLOOK 2000   OUTLOOK A-5 ◄

The page numbers are designed like a road map. Outlook indicates the Outlook section, A indicates the first unit, and 5 indicates the page within the unit.

Other Features

The two-page lesson format featured in this book provides the new user with a powerful learning experience. Additionally, this book contains the following features:

► **Real-World Case**
The case study used throughout the textbook, a fictitious company called MediaLoft, is designed to be "real-world" in nature and introduces the kinds of activities that students will encounter when working with Microsoft Outlook 2000.

► **Learning Outlook 2000 E-mail**
The Learning Outlook 2000 E-mail program features the mailbox of Alice Wegman, the marketing manager at MediaLoft. As students work through the lessons in this book, they will use Alice's account to send and receive messages, reply to and forward messages, create a Personal Distribution List, and manage a mailbox. This case scenario will help put learning into a meaningful context.

► **End of Unit Material**
Each unit concludes with a Concepts Review that tests students' understanding of what they learned in the unit. The Concepts Review is followed by a Skills Review, which provides students with additional hands-on practice of the skills. The Skills Review is followed by Independent Challenges, which pose case problems for students to solve.

Instructor's Resource Kit

The Instructor's Resource Kit is Course Technology's way of putting the resources and information needed to teach and learn effectively into your hands. With an integrated array of teaching and learning tools that offers you and your students a broad range of technology-based instructional options, we believe this kit represents the highest quality and most cutting edge resources available to instructors today. Many of these resources are available at www.course.com. The resources available with this book are:

Learning Outlook 2000 E-mail Learning Outlook 2000 E-mail is a simulation program that mimics the experiences of working with the e-mail capabilities of Microsoft Outlook 2000. Using Learning Outlook 2000 E-mail, your students will learn to send, receive, forward and reply to messages, create a Personal Distribution List, and manage a mailbox. To complete the Microsoft Outlook 2000 unit, your students must use a computer that has the Learning Outlook 2000 E-mail program installed. The Learning Outlook 2000 E-mail program is contained in the Instructor's Resource Kit. Adopters of this text are granted the right to install Learning Outlook 2000 E-mail on any stand-alone computer or network.

Instructor's Manual Available as an electronic file, the Instructor's Manual is quality-assurance tested and includes unit overviews, detailed lecture topics for each unit with teaching tips, an Upgrader's Guide, solutions to all lessons and end-of-unit material, and extra Independent Challenges. The Instructor's Manual is available on the Instructor's Resource Kit CD-ROM, or you can download it from **www.course.com**.

Course Faculty Online Companion You can browse this textbook's password-protected site to obtain the Instructor's Manual, Solution Files, Project Files, and any updates to the text. Contact your Customer Service Representative for the site address and password.

Contents

Outlook 2000

Contents

Getting
Started with Outlook 2000

Objectives

► **Understand electronic mail**
► **Start Learning Outlook 2000 E-mail**
► **View the Learning Outlook 2000 E-mail window**
► **Reading and replying to messages**
► **Create and send new messages**
► **Forward messages**
► **Manage your Inbox**
► **Create a Personal Distribution List**
► **Send a message to a Personal Distribution List**

Microsoft Outlook 2000 is an integrated desktop information management program that lets you manage your personal and business information and communicate with others. Using Outlook, you can manage information such as your electronic messages, appointments, contacts, tasks, and files. In this unit, you will focus on the electronic mail features of Outlook. You will work with a program called "Learning Outlook 2000 E-mail," a simulation program specifically designed for use with this book that looks and feels like Outlook. You will be able to use the skills learned in this unit to work with the actual Outlook program. ✎ Alice Wegman is the marketing manager at MediaLoft, a chain of eight bookstore cafés. MediaLoft sells books, CDs, and videos. Alice will use Learning Outlook 2000 E-mail to communicate with other MediaLoft employees.

Understanding Electronic Mail

Electronic mail software, popularly known as **e-mail**, is software that lets you send and receive electronic messages over a network. A **network** is a group of computers connected to each other with cables and software. Figure A-1 illustrates how e-mail messages can travel over a network. MediaLoft employees use e-mail because of its speed and ease of use. E-mail is often an effective way to communicate with co-workers or colleagues.

Following are some of the benefits of using e-mail:

 Provides a convenient and efficient way to communicate

You can send messages whenever you wish; the recipients do not have to be at their computers to receive your message. Other users can also send you electronic messages, even if you are not currently running your e-mail program. Any new messages sent to you will be waiting when you start your e-mail program.

 Allows you to send large amounts of information

Your messages can be as long as you wish, so you are not limited to the short time typically allowed on some voice mail systems. You can also attach a file (such as a spreadsheet or word processing document) to a message.

 Lets you communicate with several people at once

You can create your own electronic address book containing the names of the people with whom you frequently communicate. You can then send a message to multiple individuals at one time (without going to the copy machine first).

 Ensures delivery of information

With Outlook, you have the option of receiving a notification message when a recipient receives and reads your e-mail. To receive a notification message, the sender must be on your network and using Outlook.

 Lets you communicate from a remote place

If you have a modem and communications software, you can connect your computer at home to the computers at your office over the phone lines. This gives you the flexibility to send and receive messages when you are not at the office. You can also join a commercial online service and send e-mail to people on the **Internet**, which is a network that connects millions of computer users around the world.

 Provides a record of communications

You can organize your sent and received messages in a way that best suits your work style. Organizing your saved messages lets you keep a record of communications, which can be very valuable in managing a project or business.

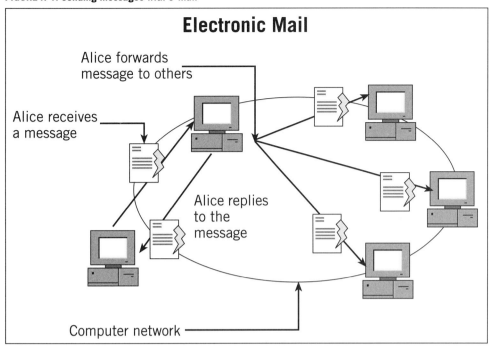

Electronic Mail

Alice forwards message to others

Alice receives a message

Alice replies to the message

Computer network

Electronic mail etiquette

When you compose a message, take extra care in what you say and how you say it. The recipient of your message doesn't have the benefit of seeing your body language or hearing the tone of your voice to interpret what you are saying. For example, using all capital letters in the text of a message is the e-mail equivalent of screaming and is not appropriate. Carefully consider the content of your messages before you send them, and don't send confidential or sensitive material. Remember, once you send a message, you may not be able to prevent it from being delivered. If your e-mail account is a company account, it's a good idea to learn whether your company permits sending personal messages. All messages you send have been legally interpreted as property of the company for which you work, so don't assume that your messages are private.

Outlook 2000

Starting Learning Outlook 2000 E-mail

Before you can read or send messages, you must start Outlook and enter a secret password. In this lesson and throughout this unit, you will work with the Learning Outlook 2000 E-mail program, which is installed in the Course Programs program group on the Start menu. (If you were using Microsoft Outlook, it would be installed in a different program group.) *You need to complete this unit in one sitting; do not exit Learning Outlook 2000 E-mail until instructed.* Alice needs to start Learning Outlook 2000 E-mail and sign into her mail account using a password.

Steps

1. **Click the Start button on the taskbar, point to Programs, then point to Course Programs**

   See Figure A-2. Note that the actual Microsoft Outlook program would be stored in a different program group on your computer.

QuickTip

Depending on how your e-mail system is set up, you may be required to follow different steps to log into your electronic mailbox.

2. **Click Learning Outlook 2000 E-mail**

   You see a message box describing the Learning Outlook 2000 E-mail simulation program.

3. **Click Continue**

   The message box describing the Learning Outlook 2000 E-mail simulation program closes, and the Learning Outlook 2000 E-mail program starts. The Enter Password dialog box appears as shown in Figure A-3. Alice Wegman is already entered as the user name. The domain name is MEDIALOFT. A **domain** is a collection of computers that the network manager groups together because the computers are used for the same task. The domain name MEDIALOFT is a fictional domain name. If this were your mail account, you would enter a mailbox name and domain name provided by your system administrator. On many networks, before you can use Outlook, you must enter a secret password identifying yourself.

4. **Click in the Password text box**

   Passwords are case sensitive; that is, *PASSWORD* is different from *password*.

QuickTip

To keep your password secret, do not write it down in a visible place, share it with others, or use a familiar or common name. Such passwords are easy for others to guess.

5. **In the Password text box, type any password you wish, using up to 19 characters, then press [Enter]**

   Four messages show up at first. After a minute, a total of nine messages appear.

CLUES TO USE

Keeping your password secure

In Learning Outlook 2000 E-mail, you can enter any password you wish using up to 19 characters. If you are on a network using Outlook, however, your system administrator will probably provide you with your own unique and secret password. After you have been assigned a password, you can then change it to one of your own choosing. It is a good idea to change your password every two months to keep it secure. Make sure you choose a password that is easy for you to remember, but difficult for others to guess. As a security benefit, your password does not appear in the Sign In dialog box as you type it. Instead, you see "*" as you type each letter.

FIGURE A-2: **Course Programs program group**

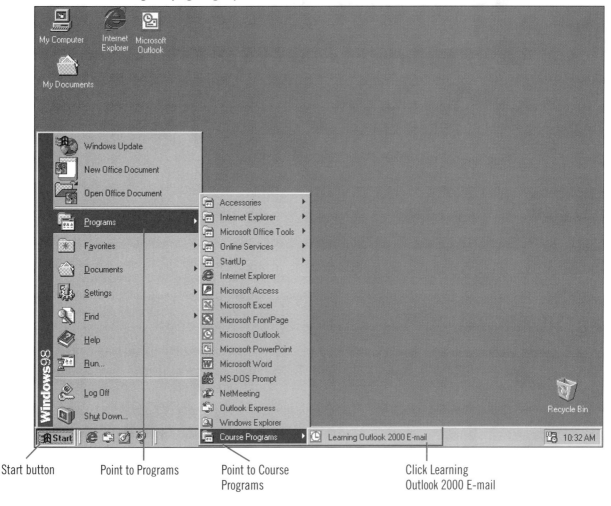

Start button | Point to Programs | Point to Course Programs | Click Learning Outlook 2000 E-mail

FIGURE A-3: **Enter Password dialog box**

Enter your password here which will appear as a series of asterisks

Viewing the Learning Outlook 2000 E-mail Window

Before you can use Outlook, you need to understand the parts of the Outlook window. Use the list below and Figure A-4 to learn about each part of the window.

 In the center of Learning Outlook 2000 E-mail window is Alice's **Inbox**, which shows a list of message headers for the e-mail she has received. Each **message header** identifies the sender of the message, the subject, and the date and time the message was received. Message headers of unread messages appear in boldface. By default, Outlook displays the Inbox with a **preview pane**, the lower pane of the Inbox. You use the preview pane to read and scroll through messages without opening them.

 Message header icons to the left of the sender's name identify the attributes of the message. For example, an icon that looks like a closed envelope indicates that the message has not been read. See Table A-1 for a description of the icons that appear in the Inbox.

 Column headings, above the message headers, identify the sections of the message header.

 On the left side of the Learning Outlook 2000 E-mail window is the **Outlook Bar**. The Outlook Bar contains shortcuts to frequently used folders. The Inbox folder is currently open. To open a different folder, you simply click the folder icon. The Inbox folder contains all the messages other users have sent you. Other folders include the Sent Items, Outbox, and Deleted Items folders. The Sent Items folder contains messages you have sent. The Outbox folder contains messages you have sent, but which Outlook has not yet delivered. The Deleted Items folder contains messages you have deleted.

 At the top of the window, the **title bar** displays the name of the program, Learning Outlook 2000 E-mail. When you are reading messages, the subject of the message appears in the title bar.

 The **menu bar** (as in all Windows programs) contains the names of the menu items. Clicking a menu item on the menu bar displays a list of related commands. For example, you use the commands on the Edit menu to edit the text of your message.

 Under the menu bar, the **toolbar** contains buttons that give you quick access to the most frequently used commands.

 Just below the toolbar, the **folder banner** displays the name of the open folder to the left and the icon of the open folder to the right.

 The **status bar** at the bottom of the window indicates the total number of messages that the open folder contains, as well as the number of those messages that have not been read.

FIGURE A-4: Learning Outlook 2000 E-mail window

Title bar
Menu bar
Toolbar
Folder banner
Message header
Inbox
Message header icon
Outlook Bar
Preview pane
Status bar

Column heading

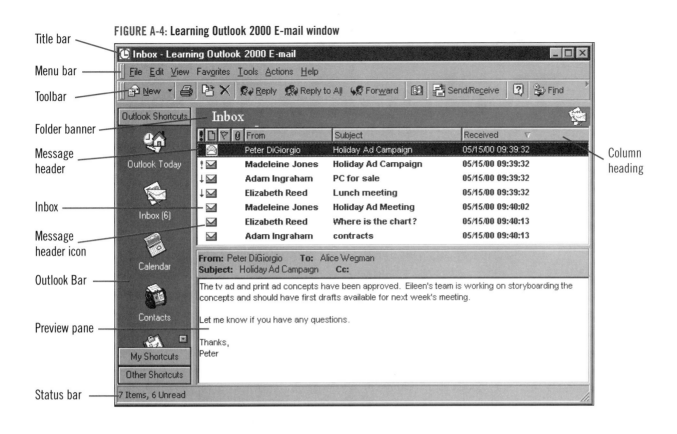

TABLE A-1: Message header icons

icon	description
↕	High importance message
↓	Low importance message
✉	Unread message
✉	Read message
✉	Forwarded message
✉	Replied to message
⊕	Notification of a delivered message
⊘	Notification of a read message
🖈	Message has an attachment
▼	Message has been flagged for follow up

Reading and Replying to Messages

To read a message in your Inbox, you can select it and then preview it in the preview pane, or you can double-click anywhere in the message header to open it in its own window. After reading a message, you can delete it, file it in another folder, or keep it in your Inbox. You can also send a response back to the sender of the message using the Reply button on the toolbar. The Reply command automatically addresses your comments to the original sender and includes the text of the original sender's message. ➤ Alice reads a few messages and sends a reply.

Steps

1. **Click the message containing Lunch meeting in the Subject column to select it, then read the message in the preview pane**
   The message appears in the lower pane of the Inbox, as shown in Figure A-5. Now you can read another message in the Inbox.

2. **Double-click the message from Madeleine Jones containing Holiday Ad Campaign in the Subject column**
   The message appears in the message window. For longer messages, it is sometimes easier to open the message in its own window. You might need to scroll to see the entire message. The yellow **InfoBar** below the message toolbar provides information about the message.

3. **Click the Reply button ✍ Reply on the message toolbar**
   A new message window appears in front of the original message window, as shown in Figure A-6, with the blinking insertion point in the message area above a copy of the original message text. The Subject text box contains the same subject as the original message.

4. **Type I prefer the Friday 4:00 time. I am working on an outline of my presentation right now and I'll send a draft to you soon. Because I will be relying on my assistant for a good part of this project, I think he should be at the meeting as well. What do you think?**

5. **Click the Send button ✉ Send on the message toolbar**
   The reply message window closes, and the reply is sent to the original sender. The InfoBar in the original message to which you replied now displays text recording the date and time that you replied to this message. See Figure A-7. In addition, Outlook stores a copy of the reply in your Sent Items folder. Messages stay in this folder until you delete them. Next, you will reply to a message that has already been read, which is indicated with an icon that looks like an opened envelope.

6. **Click the Close button ✕ in the Holiday Ad Campaign message window**
   The message window closes. In the Inbox, the icon for this message changes from the Unread message icon ✉ to the Replied to message icon ✍.

7. **Select the Holiday Ad Campaign message from Peter DiGiorgio, then click ✍ Reply**
   You do not need to open a message to reply to it. The message window appears.

8. **Type I am pleased that you are on the Holiday Ad Campaign team. I will let you know if I have any questions.**
   Your reply is entered into the message area.

9. **Click ✉ Send**
   Outlook sends the reply back to the original sender, Peter DiGiorgio, the reply message window closes, and the icon for the original message changes to ✍.

FIGURE A-5: Reading a message in the preview page

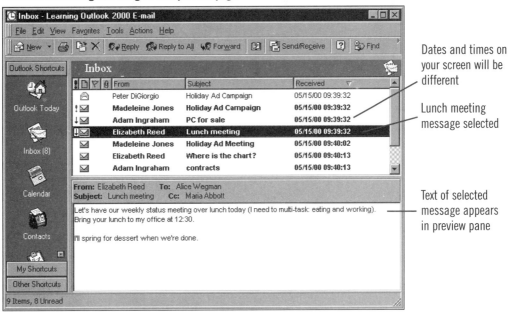

Dates and times on your screen will be different

Lunch meeting message selected

Text of selected message appears in preview pane

FIGURE A-6: Message window for replying to messages

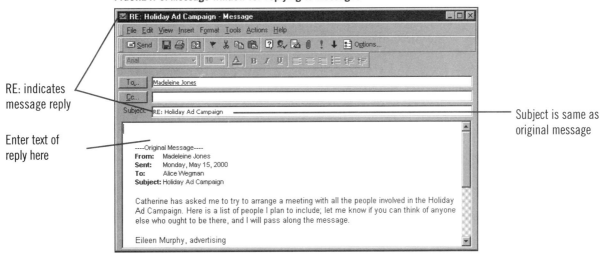

RE: indicates message reply

Enter text of reply here

Subject is same as original message

FIGURE A-7: Record of reply in replied to message

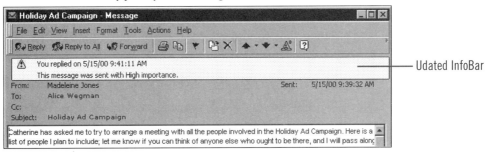

Udated InfoBar

CLUES TO USE

Emoticons

If you see something like this :-) in an e-mail message, you are looking at an emoticon. **Emoticons** are faces created by simple keyboard characters — in this example the colon, dash, and end parenthesis — to express an emotion or mood. (Turn the page sideways to see the face.) The possibilities are endless and they are a fun way to get your point across.

Creating and Sending New Messages

A critical facet of using e-mail is being able to create new messages and send them to other users on your network. When you create a message, you must indicate for whom the message is intended and specify any other recipients who should receive a copy. You also need to enter a meaningful subject for the message. Then you write the text of your message and send it. ✎ Alice wants to know if her assistant, Peter DiGiorgio, might be able to complete his assignment for the Holiday Ad Campaign earlier than originally planned, so she sends him a message. She decides to send Catherine Favreau, the Director of Advertising, a copy of this message.

1. Click the **New Mail Message button** 🖉 New on the toolbar
The new mail message window appears, as shown in Figure A-8. In this window, you enter address information and compose your message. Although you could type the information directly in the To box, to ensure that you address the message properly, you use the Address Book feature to look up the correct information.

2. Click the **Address Book button** 📖 on the new message window toolbar
The Select Names dialog box opens, as shown in Figure A-9. In this dialog box, you can view the user names of all the users connected to the mail system. These names belong to an **address book** (which is simply a collection of names and e-mail addresses) called the Global Address List. If you are not on a network, the names in this list are from your Contacts list in Outlook.

3. Scroll down and click the name **Peter DiGiorgio** to select it, then click the **To button**
The name "Peter DiGiorgio" appears in the To box in the Select Names dialog box.

4. Scroll up and click the name **Catherine Favreau**, then click the **Cc button**
The name "Catherine Favreau" appears in the Cc box (for courtesy copy).

5. Click **OK**
The Select Names dialog box closes and the new message window appears again.

6. Click in the **Subject text box**, then type **New deadline**
The text you type in the Subject box appears in the recipient's Inbox, so that the reader can quickly get an idea of the contents of the message.

7. Press **[Tab]**, then type **There is an important Holiday Ad Campaign meeting Friday, and I would like to show our ideas at that time. Let me know what I can do to facilitate your work.**
Pressing [Tab] moves the insertion point from the Subject text box to the message box.

8. Click the **Send button** ✉ Send
Outlook sends the message.

QuickTip

In the new message window, you can also click the To button or the Cc button to open the Select Names dialog box.

QuickTip

In the Select Names dialog box, double-clicking a name is a fast way to enter a name in the To box.

QuickTip

To change the way the names in the Address Book in Outlook are sorted, click the Address Book button in the Inbox window, then in the Address Book window, click View on the menu bar, point to Sort By, then click Last Name.

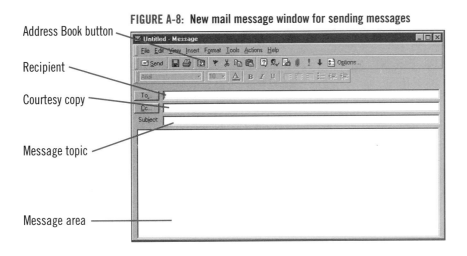

FIGURE A-8: New mail message window for sending messages

Address Book button

Recipient

Courtesy copy

Message topic

Message area

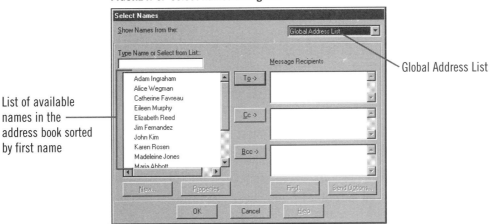

FIGURE A-9: Select Names dialog box

Global Address List

List of available names in the address book sorted by first name

CLUES TO USE

Options when sending messages

In Outlook, there are several options that affect how messages are delivered. To change these options, click the Options button [Options...] on the message toolbar to display the Message Options dialog box shown in Figure A-10. You can, for example, assign a level of importance and a level of sensitivity so that the reader can prioritize messages. You can also encrypt the message for privacy. When you want to know when a message has been received or read, you can enable the Request a delivery receipt for this message or the Request a read receipt for this message check boxes. Messages you send are automatically saved in the Sent Items folder. To have Outlook delete the messages, disable the Save sent message to check box. Examine the Message options dialog box to familiarize yourself with the other options.

FIGURE A-10: Message Options dialog box

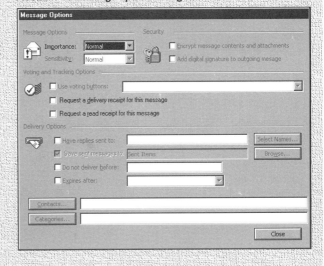

Forwarding Messages

Messages you receive from others might contain information that would be useful to someone else. With Outlook, you can forward a message to another user. The recipient of the forwarded message can then read and respond to it. ⬤▬▬ Alice has received an agenda for the Holiday Ad Campaign meeting. She would like her assistant, Peter, to attend the meeting and review the agenda before the meeting, so she forwards the message to him.

Steps 1234

1. In the Inbox window, scroll down and click the message with **Agenda** in the Subject heading, then click the **Forward button** [🔁Forward] on the toolbar
   The Forward message window appears, as shown in Figure A-11. The subject text box already contains the subject from the original message.

2. Click the **Address Book button** [📖], then scroll down and double-click the name **Peter DiGiorgio**
   The name "Peter DiGiorgio" appears in the To box in the Select Names dialog box.

3. Click **OK**
   You return to the message window. Because the subject is already completed, you continue by composing a brief introduction to the message you are forwarding.

4. Click in the message area, then type **Glad to hear you are making progress. In fact, I think you should attend Friday's meeting. Here is the agenda from Madeleine.**
   If you want to be notified when the recipient has read your message, you need to change this option before you send the message.

5. Click the **Options button** [📋Options...] on the message toolbar, then click the **Request a read receipt for this message check box**
   The Tracking option is enabled, as shown in Figure A-12.

6. Click **Close** in the Message Options dialog box, then click the **Send button** [📧Send] on the message toolbar
   The message is forwarded to Peter DiGiorgio. After a few moments you receive a notification that the forwarded message was read. This notification message is called a **read report**.

Trouble?

If your Inbox window is not maximized you will know that you have received the notification message because the screen will flicker briefly. In Outlook, the default is for new messages to appear at the top of the message list, but in this simulation, they appear at the bottom.

7. If necessary scroll down the list of messages in the Inbox window, then double-click the message from Peter DiGiorgio with the subject **Read: FW: Agenda**
   The Read message opens, as shown in Figure A-13. The Read message displays the details of the message and when it was read.

8. Click the **Close button** [✖] on the message window
   The message window closes.

FIGURE A-11: Forward message window

FW indicates the message has been forwarded

Default subject for message

Enter new text here

Text of original message

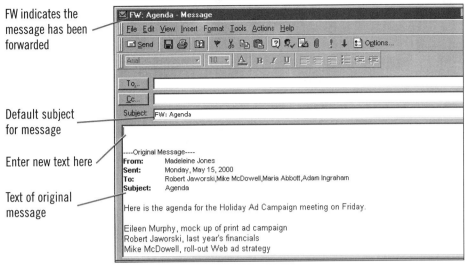

FIGURE A-12: Message Options dialog box

Request a delivery receipt for this message check box

Request a read receipt for this message check box

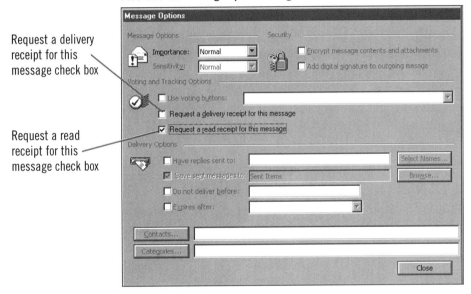

FIGURE A-13: Read Report message

Indicates Read notification message

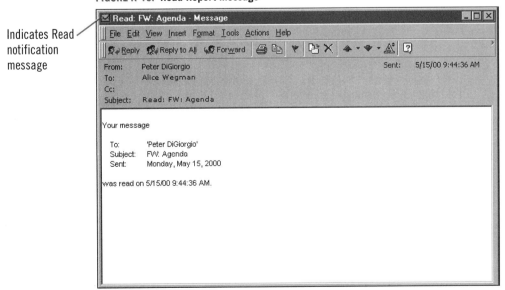

Managing Your Inbox

As you work with Outlook, the messages you receive and read accumulate in your Inbox. To keep track of important messages and prevent the Inbox from becoming too big and inefficient, Outlook offers several options. For example, you can sort messages to quickly identify the messages you need, you can print messages that you need to keep on paper, and you can delete messages you have read and no longer need. Outlook also lets you store messages in other folders, that you create. Currently the messages in the Inbox are sorted by date with the oldest message appearing at the top of the Inbox. ▟▟▟ Alice decides to clean up her Inbox by sorting the messages and deleting the messages she no longer needs. She also decides to print a message containing directions to the Holiday Ad campaign meeting.

1. Click **View** on the menu bar, point to **Current View**, click **Customize Current View**, then click **Sort**

   The Sort dialog box opens, as shown in Figure A-14.

2. Click the **Sort Items by list arrow**, then scroll up and select **From** in the list of available fields

3. Click **OK**, then click **OK** again

   The messages in the Inbox are sorted alphabetically by the sender's first name

4. Scroll up and click the message that contains **Lunch meeting** in the Subject column, then click the **Delete button** ⊠ on the toolbar

   The message is removed from the Inbox and is now stored in the Deleted Items folder. If you accidentally delete a message you intended to retain, you can open the Deleted Items folder and retrieve the message.

5. Click **View** on the menu bar, point to **Current View**, click **Customize Current View**, click **Sort**, select **Received** in the Sort Items by list box, click the **Descending option button**, click **OK** twice, then scroll to the top of the Inbox if necessary

   The newest messages appear at the top of the Inbox and the oldest messages appear at the bottom of the Inbox, as shown in Figure A-15.

6. Scroll down and click the message from Peter DiGiorgio with Holiday Ad campaign in the Subject column, then click ⊠

   It is a good idea to permanently delete all unwanted messages from the Deleted Items folder since they take up disk space.

7. Click **Tools** on the menu bar, then click **Empty "Deleted Items" Folder**

   An alert box appears, asking you to confirm that you wish to permanently delete all the items and subfolders in the Deleted Items folder.

8. Click **Yes**

   All the messages in the Deleted Items folder are permanently deleted.

9. Scroll to the top of the message list, select the **directions to meeting message** in the Inbox, click **File**, then click **Print**

   The Print dialog box opens, as shown in Figure A-16. In the actual Microsoft Outlook program, you can specify the number of copies to print and other printing options.

10. Click **OK**

    After you click OK, the dialog box closes and you return to the Inbox. Outlook prints the message on your printer.

FIGURE A-14: Sort dialog box

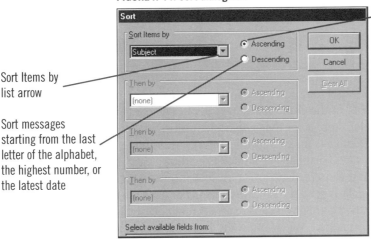

Sort Items by list arrow

Sort messages starting from the last letter of the alphabet, the highest number, or the latest date

Sort messages starting from the first letter of the alphabet, the lowest number, or the earliest date

FIGURE A-15: Messages sorted by date received

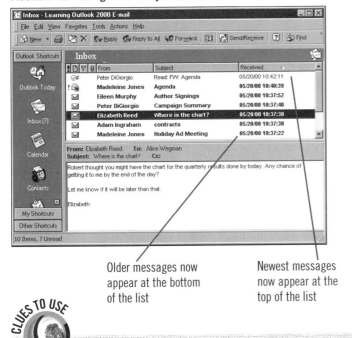

FIGURE A-16: Print dialog box

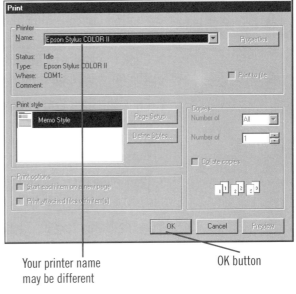

Older messages now appear at the bottom of the list

Newest messages now appear at the top of the list

Your printer name may be different

OK button

CLUES TO USE

Using folders to manage your Inbox

In the actual Outlook program you can use folders to organize your messages. On the File menu, point to New, then click Folder to create a folder to help you organize your messages. The new folder is automatically added to the folder list. To see a list of all available folders, click the folder name in the Folder banner. For example, for easy reference you might want to create a folder called "Technical" to store messages related to system procedures or using your PC. In addition, you can create folders within folders, allowing you to create a hierarchical structure for your Inbox. For instance, the "Technical" folder could contain the additional folders "Network" and "PC" so that you can further categorize your messages, as shown in Figure A-17. After creating a folder, you simply drag (or use the Cut, Copy, and Paste commands) to place messages in the desired folder.

Note that the ability to create folders is not available in the Learning Outlook 2000 E-mail program.

FIGURE A-17: Folders in Microsoft Outlook

Creating a Personal Distribution List

When you address a message, you may choose a name from a global distribution list or from the **Contacts folder** in the Outlook Address Book. The contacts folder is your e-mail address book and information storage for the people and businesses you communicate with. If there are many names in the Contacts folder, it can be time consuming to scroll through all the names to select the ones you want. Fortunately, Outlook provides an easy way to manage the user names you use most often. You can create a **Personal Distribution List**, which is a collection of contacts to whom you regularly send the same messages. For example, if you send messages reminding your staff of a weekly meeting, you can create a Personal Distribution List called "Team" that contains the names of your staff. When you want to send a message to everyone on the team, you simply select "Team" from the Select Names dialog box, instead of selecting each user name. Personal Distribution Lists are automatically added to the Contacts folder.   Alice finds that she regularly sends messages to members of her Holiday Ad Campaign team. She creates a Personal Distribution List containing these names.

Steps 1 2 3 4

1. Click the **Address Book button** 📖 on the toolbar
   The Address Book window opens.

2. Click the **New Entry button** 🗔 on the Address book toolbar
   The New Entry dialog box opens, as shown in Figure A-18. In this dialog box you can select the type of entry you want to make and in which address book the new entry will reside. Currently, there are no Personal Distribution Lists, so you need to create one.

3. Click **New Distribution List** in the Select the entry type box, then click **OK**
   The Untitled Distribution List dialog box opens, as shown in Figure A-19.

4. In the Name text box, type **Holiday Ad**, then click **Select Members**
   Outlook displays the list of names stored in the Global Address list. From this list, you select the names to include in the Holiday Ad distribution list.

Trouble?

If you accidentally click the wrong name, press and hold [Ctrl], then click the name again to deselect it.

5. Click the name **Catherine Favreau**, then press and hold [Ctrl] as you click each of the following names: **Eileen Murphy**, **Madeleine Jones** and **Peter DiGiorgio**
   With these names selected, you add them to the list.

6. Click the **Members button**
   Verify that all four names appear in the Personal Distribution List area of the dialog box, as shown in Figure A-20.

7. Click **OK**
   The Holiday Ad dialog box displays the new Holiday Ad distribution list and its members.

8. Click the **Save and Close button** in the Holiday Ad Distribution List window
   Outlook adds the Holiday Ad distribution list to the Personal Address Book in the Contacts folder.

9. Click the **Close button** ☒ in the Address Book window, then click **Contacts** in the Outlook Bar
   The contacts folder is displayed. Notice the name "Holiday Ad" in the left column.

10. Click **Inbox** in the Outlook Bar, then click **OK** in the alert box
    The Inbox folder appears again.

FIGURE A-18: New Entry dialog box

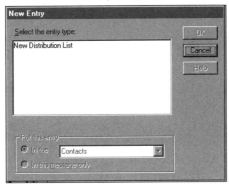

FIGURE A-19: Untitled Distribution List dialog box

Enter a name for your distribution list here

Click to add names to the list

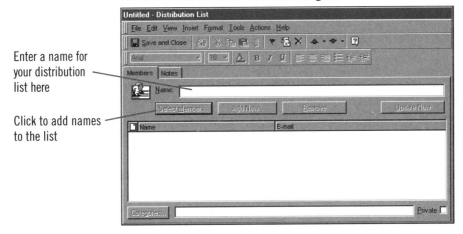

FIGURE A-20: Edit members of Holiday Ad dialog box

All four names added to distribution list

OK button

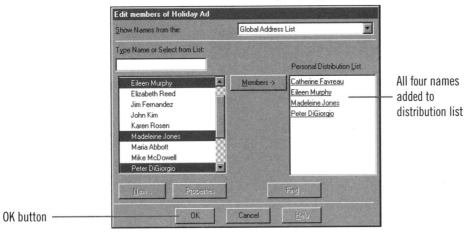

CLUES TO USE

Adding names to the Contacts folder

In Microsoft Outlook, the names of the people in your Personal Distribution Lists are automatically added to your Contacts folder, so that you can send messages to individual members without necessarily sending them to all the members of the distribution list. You can also add individual names to your Contacts folder without adding them to a distribution list. In the Address Book dialog box, click the New Entry button on the toolbar, and then double-click New Contact and enter the information for that contact. To see the contents of the Contacts folder, select Contacts in the Show names from the list box.

Unit
A

Outlook 2000

Sending a Message to a Personal Distribution List

In the same way you can send a message to an individual user, you can send a message to several users at once using a Personal Distribution List. ◀━━ Now that Alice has created a distribution list consisting of her team members, she can send a single message to all of her team using one easy-to-remember distribution list name.

Steps 1 2 3 4

1. **Click the New Mail Message button [New] on the toolbar**
   You want to send a message to all the people on the team.

2. **In the new mail message window, click the Address Book button [📖] on the message toolbar**
   Because you need to send this message to members of a Personal Distribution List, make sure you are in the Contacts folder.

3. **Click the Show Names from the list arrow, then select Contacts**
   The Contacts folder is displayed in the Select Names dialog box, as shown in Figure A-21. Outlook displays distribution list names in boldface, with the icon [📇] to the left of the name. If you had any other contacts listed, the names woud not be in boldface.

4. **Double-click Holiday Ad in the list**

5. **Click OK to return to the new mail message window**
   The To box in the new mail message window contains the Holiday Ad distribution list. Now you enter the subject of the message.

6. **Click in the Subject text box, then type No team meeting this week**
   After typing the subject of the message, you enter the text.

7. **Press [Tab], then type Because we will all be attending the Holiday Ad Campaign meeting Friday afternoon, we will not have our usual staff meeting at that time. Instead, let's get together to review the project status at 3:00 PM Thursday. Let me know if anyone has a problem with that.**

8. **Click the Send button [Send] on the message toolbar**
   Clicking this button sends the message to all the people in the Holiday Ad distribution list.
   Do not exit Learning Outlook 2000 E-mail, if you plan to complete the Skills Review.

9. **Click File on the menu bar, then click Exit to exit Learning Outlook 2000 E-mail**

FIGURE A-21: Distribution List in Contacts folder

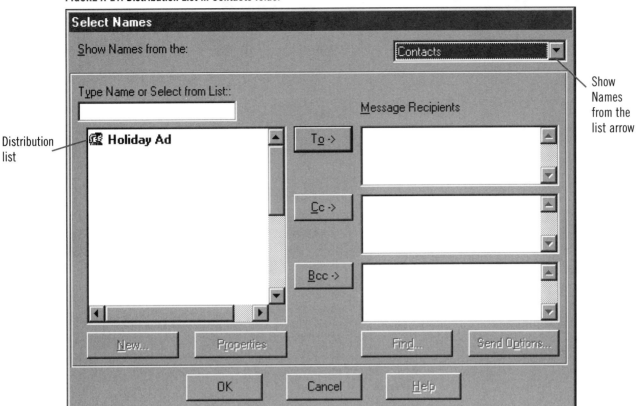

Distribution list

Show Names from the list arrow

What is Microsoft Outlook Express?

Microsoft Outlook Express is a program that you can use to exchange e-mail and join newsgroups. It comes with Windows 98. Because it focuses primarily on e-mail, it is not as robust as Outlook. Outlook comes with Microsoft Office 2000 Professional and Premium Editions. Remember that Outlook is an integrated desktop information manager that combines the Inbox function with a Calendar, Contacts database, Tasks database, and Notes database. (See the Appendix for more information on the additional features of Outlook.) However, once you learn how to use the e-mail capabilities of Outlook, you will be able to apply those skills to Outlook Express. They share many of the same menus and toolbars. For that matter, you can apply the skills you learned in this unit to any other e-mail program.

Practice

► Concepts Review

Label the elements of the Learning Outlook 2000 E-mail window shown in Figure A-22.

FIGURE A-22

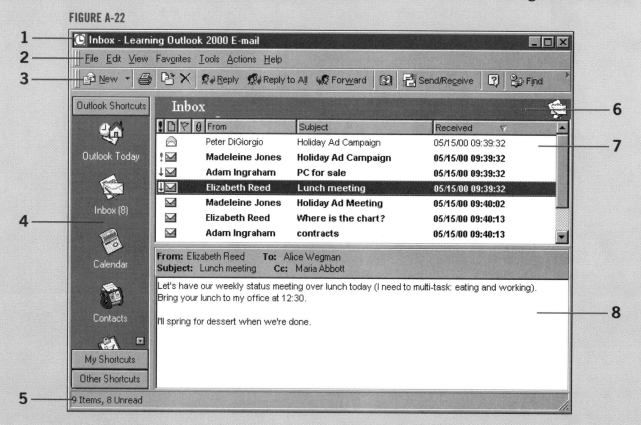

Match each term with the statement that best describes it.

9. **Electronic mail**
10. **Personal Distribution List**
11. **Contacts folder**
12. **Read report**
13. **Inbox**
14. **Message Header**

a. Stores all of the user names to whom you can send messages
b. A list of users to which you have assigned a name
c. Message you receive when someone reads the message you sent
d. Information sent and received over a computer network
e. Contains all the messages you have received
f. Identifies the sender, subject, and date of the message

Select the best answer from the list of choices.

15. A group of computers connected to each other with cables and software is called
   a. the Internet.
   b. a network.
   c. a modem.
   d. electronic mail.

16. Which of the following is the popular abbreviated name for "electronic mail"?
   a. Mail-net
   b. Electro-mail
   c. Learning Mail
   d. E-mail

17. After signing into Outlook, you see your messages in the
   a. Inbox.
   b. Message window.
   c. Mail window.
   d. Display window.

18. To read a message, you
   a. Click View, then click Read.
   b. Double-click a message.
   c. Click the Read button on the toolbar.
   d. Click the Inbox folder.

19. After reading and closing a message
   a. The next message opens so you can read it.
   b. You can click the Read button to open the next message.
   c. An icon in the message header indicates you have read the message.
   d. The message is automatically deleted from the Inbox.

20. To forward a selected message to another user, you
   a. Click File, then click Forward.
   b. Click the Forward button.
   c. Click the Send button.
   d. Click Tools, then click Forward.

21. To create a new message, you
   a. Click the New Mail Message button.
   b. Click the Create button.
   c. Click the Mail button.
   d. Click the Send button.

22. To send the same message to multiple recipients, which of the following is *not* an option?
   a. Drag the message to each of the recipient names
   b. In the Select Names dialog box, you can select multiple names from the Contacts folder
   c. You can enter multiple names in the To box
   d. Create a Personal Distribution List containing the names of the users

► Skills Review

If you exited from the Learning Outlook 2000 E-mail program before continuing on to this Skills Review, you will need to practice sending and deleting a few messages before you continue. You do not need to perform these steps if you did not exit Learning Outlook 2000 E-mail at the end of the unit.

1. Start Learning Outlook 2000 E-mail.
2. Send three different messages to any three different users.
3. Delete any two messages from any two users.
4. Send one more message to any user.

After a minute or so, the messages described in the Skills Review exercises will begin to appear, so you can continue.

1. **Read and reply to messages.**
   a. Double-click the message containing "contracts" in the Subject column.
   b. Click the Close button in the message window.
   c. Double-click the message containing "Author Signings" in the Subject column.
   d. Click the Reply button on the message toolbar.
   e. Type "Stephen King lives on the East Coast and might be interested. Can't hurt to start big! Let me know how it goes."
   f. Click the Send button on the Reply message toolbar.
   g. Click the Close button in the message window.

2. **Create and send new messages.**
   a. Click the New Mail Message button on the toolbar.
   b. Click the Address Book button on the message toolbar.
   c. Click the name "Peter DiGiorgio" to select it, then click the To button.
   d. Click the name "Elizabeth Reed," then click the Cc button.
   e. Click OK.
   f. Type "New chart" in the Subject text box.
   g. Press [Tab] and type "I think the Results chart for Elizabeth should include a pie chart as well as a bar graph."
   h. Click the Send button in the message toolbar.

3. **Forward a message.**
   a. In the Inbox window, double-click the message with "Where is the chart?" in the Subject heading, then click the Forward button on the toolbar.
   b. Click the Address Book button, then double-click the name "Peter DiGiorgio."
   c. Click OK.
   d. Click the insertion point in the message area and type "Glad to hear you are making progress on the charts. I am passing along a message from Elizabeth. You can respond directly to her."
   e. Click the Options button, click the Request a read receipt for this message check box, then click close.
   f. Click the Send button in the Forward message toolbar.
   g. Click the Close button in the message window.
   h. Double-click the message from Peter DiGiorgio with the subject "Read: FW: Where is the chart?"
   i. Click the Close button in the message window.

4. Manage your Inbox.

   a. Click View on the menu bar, point to Current View, click Customize Current View, then click Sort.

   b. Click the Sort Items by list arrow, click From, click the Descending option button, then click OK twice.

   c. Click the message that contains "Holiday Ad Meeting" in the Subject column and click the Delete button on the toolbar.

   d. Click View on the menu bar, point to Current View, click Customize Current View, then click Sort.

   e. Click the Sort Items by list arrow, select Importance, click the Descending option button, then click OK twice.

   f. Click the message that contains "Agenda" in the Subject column, click File on the menu bar, then click Print.

   g. Click OK.

5. Create a Personal Distribution List.

   a. Click the Address Book button.

   b. Click the New Entry button on the Address Book toolbar.

   c. Click New Distribution List in the Select the entry type box, then click OK.

   d. In the Name box, type Systems Committee, then click Select Members.

   e. Click Robert Jaworski, then choose the following names by pressing [Ctrl] as you click each name: Madeleine Jones, Adam Ingraham.

   f. Click the Members button.

   g. Click OK.

   h. Click the Save and Close button on the message toolbar.

   i. Click the Close button in the Address Book window.

6. Send a message to a Personal Distribution List.

   a. Click the New Mail Message button.

   b. In the new mail message window, click the Address Book button.

   c. Click the Show Names from the list arrow, then click contacts.

   d. Double-click "Systems Committee" from the list.

   e. Click OK.

   f. In the Subject text box, type "Next systems meeting."

   g. In the message area, type "At next Thursday's meeting, we will review the proposals from the training companies. Please come prepared to defend your preferences."

   h. Click Send.

If you have been assigned Independent Challenge 1, do not exit the Learning Outlook 2000 E-mail program before continuing.

► Independent Challenges

In Order to complete Independent Challenge 1, you must have completed the Skills Review.

1. To help you become more comfortable using the Outlook program, you can start the part of the Learning Outlook 2000 E-mail program that is designed to give you the freedom to experiment with Outlook features and procedures. After you complete the Skills Review, you will receive a number of messages at random in your Inbox.
To complete this independent challenge:

a. Reply to, forward, delete, sort, and print these new messages.
b. Create and send new messages of your own.
c. Explore using the different send options described in this unit.
d. Click File, then click Exit to exit Learning Outlook 2000 E-mail.

2. If you have access to Microsoft Outlook 2000 or any other e-mail program, you can apply the skills you've learned in this unit (working with the simulation) to the actual program.
To complete this independent challenge:

a. Send a message (composed of any text) with a high priority to any user in your Contacts folder.
b. Reply to a message that was sent to you.
c. Forward a message to another user.
d. Delete a message you don't need anymore.
e. Create a Personal Distribution List called "Jokes" that you will use to forward jokes that you receive.
f. Print the high priority message that you sent in Step A. This should now reside in your Sent Items folder.

Appendix

Beyond E-mail: Understanding Additional Outlook Features

Objectives

▶ **Manage your appointments and tasks**
▶ **Manage your contacts**
▶ **Preview your day**

To effectively use Microsoft Outlook 2000 in managing your business and personal information, it is important to know not only how to use the Inbox to send and receive electronic messages, but also how to use the additional components in Outlook. Outlook integrates several tools, including Inbox, Calendar, Contacts, Tasks, Notes, and Outlook Today to provide you with a uniquely comprehensive information manager.

Now that you know how to manage your electronic messages with Inbox, you will learn how Outlook combines e-mail with its other components to create a new class of program: an integrated desktop information manager.

Managing Your Appointments and Tasks

The Calendar and Tasks tools in Microsoft Outlook provide convenient, effective means to manage your appointments and tasks. **Calendar** is the electronic equivalent of your desk calendar, while **Tasks** is an electronic to-do list. Calendar defines an **appointment** as an activity that does not involve inviting other people or scheduling resources; a **meeting** as an activity you invite people to or reserve resources for; and an **event** as an activity that lasts 24 hours or longer. You can specify the subject and location of the activity, and its start and end times. You can also ensure that you do not forget the activity by having Outlook sound a reminder prior to the start of the activity. Outlook will notify you if the activity conflicts with, or is adjacent to, another scheduled activity. You can view any period of time that you desire in Calendar. For example, you can look at and plan activities for next month or even next year.

Details

Review the following features of Calendar and Tasks:

 To schedule your appointments, meetings, and events, open the **Outlook Shortcuts** on the Outlook Bar, click the **Calendar folder**, and then click the **New Appointment button** on the toolbar. See Figure AP-1. To make your screen match the figure, click View on the menu bar, point to CurrentView, click Day/Week/Month, then click the Day button on the toolbar.

 To facilitate planning and scheduling your activities, you can choose to view Calendar by day, week, or month, and you can use the **Date Navigator** to quickly select even nonadjacent days. Dates displayed in boldface on the Date Navigator indicate days on which you have scheduled appointments.

 Use Calendar to schedule a meeting by having Outlook check the availability of all the invitees internally as well as over the Internet. Once you have selected a meeting time and location, you can send invitations in meeting requests. If the invitee accepts the invitation, Outlook will post the meeting automatically to the invitee's calendar.

 Save Calendar as an HTML file to publish it over the Web. It can then be shared over a corporate **intranet** (an internal internet) or over the Internet to aid others in working with your schedule.

 To manage your business and personal to-do list, open the **Tasks folder** on the Outlook bar. See Figure AP-2.

 Click the **New Task button** to create new tasks. Once you create a task, you can work with that task in several ways. Click the **Organize button** to organize your tasks by grouping them in **categories** such as ideas or competition. View your tasks in several different ways, including by subject, by status, and by due date. You can mark your progress on tasks by percentage complete, and you can have Outlook create status summary reports in e-mail messages and then send the update to anyone on the update list.

 Use the **New Task Request** command on the Actions menu to assign tasks to a co-worker or assistant and have Outlook automatically update you on the status of the task completion. To help you coordinate your tasks and your appointments, the task list from Tasks is automatically displayed in the **TaskPad** in Calendar. To schedule time to complete a task, simply drag a task from the TaskPad to a time block in the Calendar. Any changes you make to a task are reflected in both the TaskPad in Calendar and the task list in Tasks.

 If you want to quickly write down an idea or a note concerning an appointment or a task, simply open the **Notes folder** on the Outlook bar and click the **New Note button** on the toolbar. See Figure AP-3. **Notes** is the electronic version of the popular colored paper sticky notes.

FIGURE AP-1: Appointments, meetings, and events displayed in the Calendar window

New Appointment button

Outlook Bar

Calendar folder

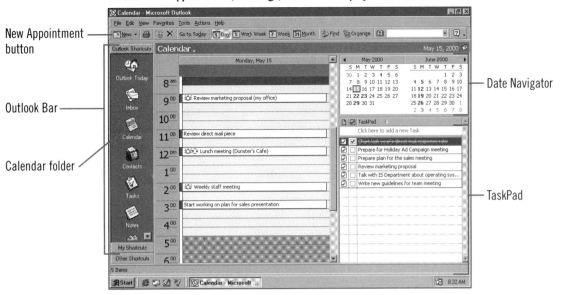

Date Navigator

TaskPad

FIGURE AP-2: Tasks list displayed in the Tasks window

New Task button

Organize button

Tasks organized by category

Tasks folder

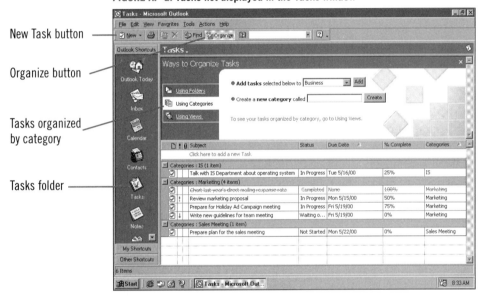

FIGURE AP-3: Notes displayed in the Notes window

New Note button

Notes folder

Managing Your Contacts

The **Contacts** tool in Microsoft Outlook enables you to manage all your business and personal contact information. With Contacts, you can store each contact's general information such as full name, company, job title, as well as up to three street addresses, three e-mail addresses, and more than a dozen telephone numbers. You also can store each contact's Web page address.

Review the following features of Contacts:

 To open Contacts, click the **Contacts folder** in the Outlook group on the Outlook Bar. See Figure AP-4. Click the **New Contact button** on the toolbar to enter new contact information and to begin using the Contacts features.

 Click the **Full Name button** to enter the full name for the contact, including title, first name, middle name, last name, and suffix if appropriate. See Figure AP-5. You can easily sort and group your contacts by any part of their names.

 Click the **Address button** to enter an address for a contact. The address can include the street, city, state/province, postal code, and country/region. Click the **Details tab** to store each contact's detailed information, including the department or office in which he or she works, the assistant's or manager's name, the contact's birthday, anniversary, or even the contact's nickname. In addition, to facilitate finding a contact quickly, Outlook allows you to file each contact under any name that you choose, including under a first name, a last name, a company name, or any word such as "architect" or "caterer." Outlook will automatically present you with several naming options under which to file each contact, but you are free to choose any word you like. Once you have entered your contacts' information, you can view your contacts in a variety of ways, including as detailed address cards, as a phone list, or by company, category, or location.

 If you have a modem, use automatic dialing to quickly dial a contact telephone number. Click the **Dial button** on the Contacts toolbar, select a contact, click **Start Call**, click **Dialing Options**, click **Line Properties**, then select the modem and connections options you want on the General, Connections and Options tabs. After Outlook has dialed the phone number, pick up the phone handset and click **Talk**.

 Keep track of all e-mail, tasks, appointments, and documents relating to a specific contact by linking any item or document to a contact. For example, when you create a new Microsoft Outlook item, such as a task, you can link it to the contact to which it relates. You can also link any items that already exist in folders to a contact. And, you can link documents to a contact. For more information on these features, refer to Microsoft Outlook Help and enter the phrase **linking an item to a contact**.

 Send contact information over the Internet by using Internet **vCards**, the Internet standard for creating and sharing virtual business cards. You can save a contact as a save vCards sent in e-mail messages. To send a vCard to someone in e-mail, click **Contacts**, click the contact you want to send as a vCard, click **Actions**, and then click **Forward as vCard**.

 If you want to create a mailing list that's a subset of your Contacts folder, you can filter the Contacts list and then use the filtered list to begin a mail merge from Outlook. When you **filter** a list, you search for only specific information—for example, only those contacts that live in Kansas. You can create a variety of merged documents in Microsoft Word, and you can begin your mail merge from Outlook. You can create form letters, print mailing labels, or print addresses on envelopes. You can also send bulk e-mail messages or faxes to your contacts. To send a mail merge to a filtered set of your contacts, click the **View menu** in Contacts, point to **Current View**, and then click **Customize Current View**. Click **Filter** and then select the options you want. Once you have the view created, start the mail merge by clicking **Mail Merge** on the Tools menu.

FIGURE AP-4: Contacts displayed in the Contacts window

New Contact button

Dial button

Contacts folder

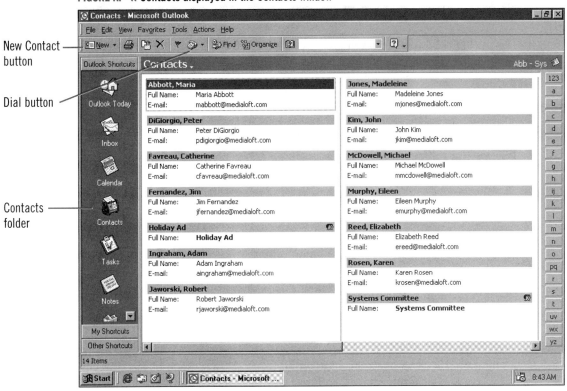

FIGURE AP-5: Individual contact in the Contact dialog box

Details tab

Full Name button

Address button

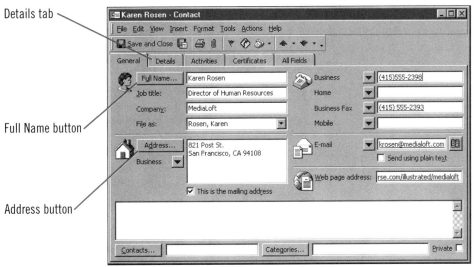

Previewing Your Day

The **Outlook Today page** provides a preview of your day at a glance. It is the electronic version of your day planner book and provides a snapshot view of the activities, tasks, contacts, and notes that you've entered into various Outlook tools. Just as with a paper-based daily planner, you can customize how you view Outlook Today to fit your personal style and work habits. See Figure AP-6.

Details

Review the following features of Outlook Today:

 View how many messages are in your Inbox, Outbox, and Drafts folders. The right pane of Outlook Today displays your message information. You can customize Outlook Today to show any of your Personal Folders in the Messages pane.

 Outlook allows you to view your appointments over the next few days. These appear in the Calendar section of Outlook Today, which is located in the left pane. You can choose to show anywhere from 1–7 days of appointments and tasks in your Calendar.

 Tasks appear in the center pane of Outlook Today, allowing you to list all of your tasks in one convenient place. You can customize Outlook Today to show all your tasks or just today's tasks. You can also sort your tasks by Importance, Due Date, Creation Time, or Start Date, and in ascending or descending order. In addition, you can keep track of tasks by checking off task items that you've accomplished. You can click the checkbox to the left of the task to indicate you've completed it. The task list will be updated automatically in the Tasks folder.

 For detailed information on a Calendar item, you can double-click the appointment or meeting. Clicking the appointment or meeting opens the Appointment or Meeting dialog box. You can see more details at a glance and then close the dialog box to view Outlook Today again.

 Customize the page for the way you work by clicking the **Customize Outlook Today button** in the Outlook Today window. You can change the tasks that appear on the Outlook Today page, change how many appointments appear on the Outlook Today page, determine from where e-mail messages are sent and received, and change the style of Outlook Today (how it looks). You can also make the Outlook Today page your default page when you start Outlook.

FIGURE AP-6: Outlook Today page

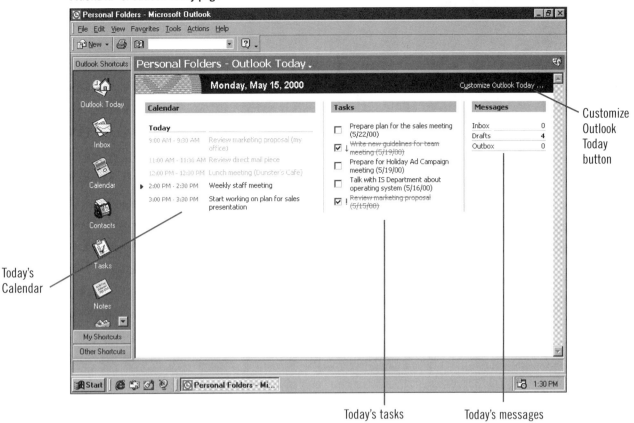

Today's
Calendar

Customize
Outlook
Today
button

Today's tasks   Today's messages

Outlook 2000

Practice

► Concepts Review

Label the elements of the calendar window shown in Figure AP-7.

FIGURE AP-7

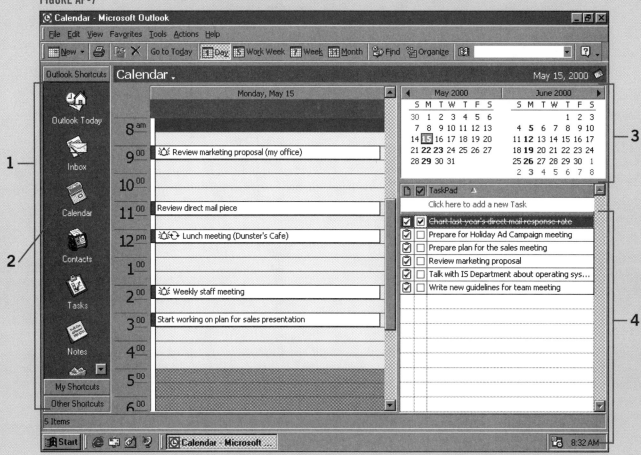

Select the best answer from the list of choices.

5. Which of the following is *not* one of the Outlook tools:
   a. Inbox   **b.** Meeting Planner   **c.** Calendar   **d.** Notes

6. Use the _____ feature to schedule your appointments, meetings, and events.
   a. Calendar   **b.** Tasks   **c.** Notes   **d.** Contacts

7. Use the _____ feature to manage your business and personal to-do list.
   a. Calendar   **b.** Tasks   **c.** Notes   **d.** Contacts

8. Use the _____ feature to supplement the information stored in Calendar and Tasks.
   a. Calendar   **b.** Tasks   **c.** Notes   **d.** Contacts

Glossary

Outlook 2000

Address book A collection of user names.

Appointment An activity that does not involve inviting other people or scheduling resources.

Calendar A tool within Outlook that is the electronic equivalent of your daily desk calendar.

Categories A method for organizing your tasks.

Computer network Two or more connected computers that can share information and resources.

Contacts A tool in Outlook that enables you to manage all your business and personal contact information.

Contacts folder A feature of Contacts that allows you to view, edit, and create contacts.

Date Navigator A feature in Calendar that allows you to quickly select even, nonadjacent days.

Deleted Items folder A folder in the Inbox folder that contains messages you have deleted.

Details tab A tab in the Contact dialog box used to store each contact's detailed information.

E-mail Electronic mail software that lets you send and receive electronic messages over a network.

Emoticons Faces created by simple keyboard characters to express an emotion or mood.

Event An activity that lasts 24 hours or longer.

Filter To search for specific information.

Folder banner The horizontal bar that indicates the name of the open folder to the left and the icon of the open folder to the right.

Global Address List An address book that contains all the user names of the people connected to the mail system.

Inbox Part of the e-mail window that contains the e-mail you have received.

Internet A communication system that connects computers and computer networks located around the world using telephone lines, cables, satellites, and other telecommunications media.

Learning Outlook 2000 E-mail Software that simulates the look and functionality of Microsoft Outlook 2000.

Meeting An activity you invite people to or reserve resources for.

Message header The area at the top of a message that identifies the sender of the message, the subject, and the date and time the message was received.

Network A group of computers connected to each other with cables and software to allow users to share applications, disk storage, printers, and send and receive electronic messages from one another.

Notes A tool in Outlook that is an electronic version of the popular colored paper sticky notes.

Notes folder A feature in Notes that allows you to quickly write down an idea or a note concerning an appointment or task.

Outbox folder A folder in the Inbox folder that contains messages you have sent, but which Outlook has not yet delivered.

Outlook bar The bar located on the left side of the e-mail window that contains shortcuts to frequently used folders.

Outlook Express An Internet Explorer suite component that allows you to exchange e-mail and join newsgroups.

Outlook Today page A tool within Outlook that provides a preview of your day at a glance.

Personal Distribution List A collection of contacts to whom you regularly send the same messages.

Preview pane The lower pane of the Inbox that allows you to read and scroll through your messages without opening them.

Report message A message you receive when the e-mail recipient either receives or opens a message you sent.

Sent Items folder A folder in the Inbox folder that contains messages you have sent.

Status bar The bar at the bottom of the Outlook window that indicates the total number of messages that the open folder contains, as well as the number of those messages that have not been read.

TaskPad An area in Calendar that displays your task list.

Task requests A feature in Tasks that allows you to assign tasks to co-workers or assistants and have Outlook automatically update you on the status of task completion.

Tasks A tool within Outlook that is an electronic to-do list.

Tasks folder A feature in Tasks that allows you to manage your business and personal to-do list.

Vcards The Internet standard for creating and sharing virtual business cards.

Outlook 2000

Index

Index

▶P

passwords
 security of, Outlook A-4

Password text box, Outlook A-4

Personal Distribution List, Outlook A-16–17
 sending e-mail messages to, Outlook A-18–19

preview pane, Outlook A-6–7

Print dialog box, Outlook A-14–15

printing
 e-mail messages, Outlook A-14

priority options
 for e-mail messages, Outlook A-11

▶R

read receipts
 for e-mail messages, Outlook A-11

Reply button, Outlook A-8–9

replying to e-mail messages, Outlook A-8–9

▶S

security
 of passwords, Outlook A-4

Select Names dialog box, Outlook A-10

Send button, Outlook A-8–9, Outlook A-10

sending e-mail messages, Outlook A-10–11

Sort dialog box, Outlook A-14–15

sorting
 Address Book entries, Outlook A-10
 e-mail messages, Outlook A-14

Start button, Outlook A-4

Start Call option, Outlook AP-4

status bar, Outlook A-6–7

▶T

Talk option, Outlook AP-4

TaskPad, Outlook AP-2

tasks
 in Outlook Today, Outlook AP-6–7

Tasks folder, Outlook AP-2–3

Tasks tool, Outlook AP-2–3

title bar, Outlook A-6–7

toolbars, Outlook A-6–7

Tracking option, Outlook A-12–13